JOURNEY INTO VARANASI

by Roger Hooker

To the memory of my father-in law,
Max Warren,
in gratitude and great affection.

By the same author
UNCHARTED JOURNEY

CHURCH MISSIONARY SOCIETY

© 1978

ISBN 0 85273 022 5

Cover designed by Chris Beales
Printed by Stanley L. Hunt (Printers) Ltd
Midland Road, Rushden, Northants

CONTENTS

FOREWORD

by the Bishop of Guildford

A recent Roman Catholic survey of the world scene ended with these words: "by a providential coincidence with world events, a new Pentecostal wind is sweeping through the Church which has never faced a greater challenge and never had a better opportunity to become Church for the world". (From *The Coming of the Third Church* by Walbert Bühlmann, St Paul Publications, Slough, 1974. p. 407.)

In our Western churches, people are becoming aware of that opportunity. Until a few years ago it was possible for us to visualise missionary work as crossing geographical boundaries to plant the church in new areas where there had never before been any Christians. That has now changed and there are few geographical boundaries to cross in that way. Although often few in numbers, Christian churches exist in every country of the world, and in almost every major city. This great new fact of Christian mission is slowly coming home to us through the work of the World Council of Churches and other international bodies like the Anglican Consultative Council. The churches are in partnership for world mission.

New opportunities, however, bring new challenges and one of the most important is learning how to respond to the pluralist nature of modern societies and how to witness within them. In Britain, as in other countries of Western Europe, we are learning to share citizenship with people who come from African or Asian backgrounds, or who practice another religion, Islam, Hinduism or Buddhism. We are discovering that they also have treasures and wisdom to share with us and that true community can only be built and sustained when every separate group within it has freedom to be true to itself, and to contribute to the life of the whole. Good relationships between the cultural and religious groups in Britain have become a major issue on our national agenda.

The situation of pluralism is a novel one for Christians in Britain, but not for Christians in the Middle East, in Africa or in Asia. The ancient churches of the Middle East have lived amongst Muslim majorities for centuries, while in Africa and Asia many nation states are built on the common loyalty of people from two or more major religions. Pluralism is an important characteristic of the new period of human history which has come with the technological advance and the changed circumstances of the twentieth century. Mankind is faced with the challenge of building one world community and it is clear that this can only be achieved if it is accepted that such a community will be pluralist in character, joining together people of different ethnic origins, cultures and religions in mutual trust and in a common enterprise.

It is important, therefore, that people of different religions should understand each other in as sympathetic and imaginative way as possible. The text books of comparative religion set out the facts about beliefs and practices, but they need supplementing by more personal accounts of journeys across the boundaries between different cultures and religions. We understand others best when we have a testimony of friendship to help us appreciate their hidden strengths, the integrity of their motives and the intensity of their feelings: friendship helps us to see with our friend's eyes, from the place where he himself stands. And what is true of individuals is true also of groups of people.

We do not all have the privilege of friendship with people who profess another faith, and we must often rely on the experience of those who have. They can be for us bridge-builders, helping us to cross the barriers of misunderstanding, of strangeness, of prejudice, and to see what life is like on the other side. Roger Hooker's book is just such a bridge. It grows out of his experience while studying Sanskrit at the Sanskrit University of Varanasi, but it distils much more than the lessons learnt on the campus. It reflects the wide range of contacts with Hindus, Buddhists and Muslims which Roger developed as he and his family lived quietly and modestly amongst them, with perceptive minds and receptive hearts. Kenneth Cragg pioneered this form of writing in his *The Call of the Minaret*, and Roger's book stands in that succession. Beginning with a sensitive analysis of the landmarks which guide the enquirer who seeks to appreciate the Hindu attitude to life, he goes on to explain the attitudes which make that appreciation possible. The patience, integrity and innocence of which he speaks are needed by all who seek to build good human relations in a pluralistic society.

Christians look beyond the next chapter of human history, when people of every faith and none must learn to live in community with those who differ from them, to the End when "the universe, all in heaven and on earth, is brought into a unity in Christ" (*Ephesians* 1.10).

That fulfilment, however, lies in the hands of God, and we affirm it now only by faith and in hope. For the moment our task is to build true community with others in the pluralist society which is modern Britain. Roger's sensitive reflections on his service of Christ's presence in Varanasi will help us all to do our task better, and to do it with our hope set on Christ's fulfilment. I hope that many will read and study it with care.

David Brown
(Bishop of Guildford)

Preface

This book is the fruit of 13 years spent in India and in particular of the last six which were spent in the holy city of Varanasi (Benares). It is a record of personal experience: I have described something of my efforts to gain an entrance into educated Hindu society, and to discover a way of obedience to my missionary vocation in that context. It is my conviction that our Christian discussion about other faiths must be firmly rooted at this personal level. It cannot remain here, but here it must begin.

Like any other, this approach has its own inbuilt limitations. I would draw particular attention to two: first, my experience was confined to a small area of north India. I make no claim to generalise from this basis about other parts of that vast and richly varied sub-continent. I make this important qualification here in order to avoid distracting the reader's attention by repeating it every time I use the words Hindu or Hinduism in the body of the book. Second, my approach is inevitably and properly conditioned by my cultural background, and by the particular part of the Christian family to which I belong. Other approaches by missionaries who come from different backgrounds are as valid as they are urgently necessary.

I owe a great deal to the generous and patient friendship

of many people in Varanasi, and especially to those who shared with me the very personal accounts described in chapter four. In each case they have read what I have written about them, checked it for accuracy, and given their consent to its publication in this book. I am particularly grateful to Dr Satya Prakash Mittal of the Institute of Gandhian Studies, and to Professor Krishna Nath of Kashi Vidyapith University, Varanasi, both of whom read the whole typescript and assured me that I had written nothing about Hinduism which they found objectionable or incorrect—though this of course is in no way to suggest that they would agree with the argument.

Last, I must record, though I cannot adequately describe or discharge, the debt I owe the person to whose memory this book is dedicated. My ministry in India was a partnership with him, for we discussed it and shared it in a weekly correspondence which lasted almost unbroken from 1965 until his death in 1977. In the last letter he wrote to me he gave his blessing on the first draft of this book. While responsibility for all that appears in it is mine, the inspiration for it, as for so much else, was his. My hope and prayer is that it may be a small contribution to our contemporary obedience to that great commission in whose service his own life was so gladly and gloriously spent.

Roger Hooker
September 1977

11

Chapter 1

LOOKING FOR LANDMARKS

For the newcomer Varanasi can be a disconcerting place. The old part of the city is a maze of narrow lanes in which he very quickly loses his way. If he asks how to get to a certain place he will often receive just a vague wave of the hand. If he asks someone else a few minutes later he may be told to go in the opposite direction, and after a little while he is reduced to a state of helpless frustration.

Yet there is another way of exploring the city. Instead of setting out for one particular place he can deliberately lose himself among the lanes. If he is prepared to take his time he discovers that though Hindus may seem to be poor guides to hurrying Englishmen with one-track minds they can be delightful companions to someone who is prepared to stop and talk with them. Frustration gives place to fascination.

After doing this several times the explorer finds that he is learning to find his way around the lanes without really trying, for the landmarks begin to stand out, and with their aid he can chart his course.

Exploring Hinduism is strangely like exploring the most sacred city of the Hindus. The western mind functions logically, moving forward step by step. In matters of faith we often want to be clear and definite and we call this, significantly, knowing where we stand. It is therefore disconcerting to find that a Hindu can hold apparently contradictory beliefs without any sense of incongruity. For example he believes that after death the soul goes to one of the many heavens or hells where it is repaid for the good or evil deeds it has done on earth, before returning to earth to be reborn for another life. Yet he also believes that it is in this new life itself that the soul must work out the entail of its past actions, and this seems to make the heavens and hells superfluous. Again, he may be a devout worshipper of God or an avowed atheist, yet he is still a Hindu either way. It is not surprising that many a westerner has set out to understand Hinduism and then given up the attempt in despair.

Yet there is another way. Instead of trying to understand in a logical way one can, so to speak, deliberately lose oneself in Hinduism. This means talking with people, visiting places, dipping into books and magazines, and not worrying at how little sense it all appears to make, but simply being prepared to relax, to absorb and to attend—an attitude which bears a family likeness to contemplative prayer. Hindus are sensitive to mood and empathy and are very ready to talk with someone in whom they can detect this attitude. When one has been doing this for a while one notices that certain words and ideas are repeated. They seem to come into every conversation and every book. Often they are baffling, like the constant refrain that 'all religions say the same thing'. Sometimes it is not words but gestures and attitudes towards others that one notices again and again. These are the landmarks which slowly begin to stand out from the surrounding confusion. Then one begins to see that these landmarks are related to one another, and so slowly Hinduism and Hindus become a little less baffling.

For the missionary this process is the indispensable foundation of all he tries to do, for until one can discern some of the landmarks in the country of another person's mind genuine communication is impossible, though India's unfailing courtesy has often concealed this state of affairs from insensitive foreigners.

14

What then are the main landmarks of Hinduism? Here I describe three from among the many which have come to seem important to me.

1. Soon after arriving in Varanasi I attended a lecture by a Hindu scholar on *Man in Vedanta Philosophy*. He began by saying: "Man longs for happiness. He cannot find this in transient phenomena which are subject to change and decay. He knows he can only find it in what is permanent, and this he finds in consciousness." Man's search for permanent happiness and its corollary, the desire to escape from pain and sorrow, is a very common starting point for books and popular addresses on Hindu philosophy and spirituality. This search is one which ought to win an echo of sympathy from the heart of the Christian for the experience from which it springs is universal. "Change and decay in all around I see. . ." Vedanta philosophy predominates among the educated in north India, while the uneducated are familiar with and live by its major tenets. According to this philosophy the fulfilment of man's quest for permanence is found in the absorption of his limited individual consciousness in that universal consciousness of which it is a part, as a drop of water is absorbed in the ocean. The biggest obstacle in the way of reaching this goal is the individual's mistaken awareness of his own separate identity. A frequent refrain of the Hindu scriptures and of Hindus themselves is that we must get rid of "the sense of me and mine".

When the Christian first meets this notion he finds it either meaningless or repellent and so he is apt to shy away from it, yet he must try to grasp its inner meaning for it lies at the heart of the Hindu vision of things. Hindus will tell him that it can never be understood by rational thought but only realised after a long period of disciplined meditation, in a state of bliss which transcends all mental concepts.

Yet one comes across experiences in other areas of life which seem to bear a close resemblance to this. For example, in classical Sanskrit drama which flourished in court circles a thousand years and more ago, the aim was to create certain emotions in which all the audience could share, each

15

spectator transcending his own separateness in a common experience which was always held to be one of blissful joy. This meant that the characters of the drama were not distinctive personalities in the western sense but rather stylised figures through whom the appropriate mood could be created, and indeed they could all be fitted into one or other of a small number of fixed categories.

A similar example occurs in the world of scholarship. A young Sanskrit scholar once said to me: "I have studied Hindu and Buddhist philosophy, but now I am no longer interested in separate 'isms', I want to work on a unity of these two philosophies." This is a very typical remark. To stay on the level of separate religions and philosophies is to be locked in narrowness, dogmatism and conflict: "This is my religion, that is your religion." This is comparable to the individual's urge to keep his own identity, his sense of me and mine. The result is that religions can only meet in the bitterness and barrenness of mutual repudiation and anathema, or else be absorbed into a unity in which their distinctiveness is lost.

Thus the Christian who talks with a Hindu finds at the very outset that he is expected to renounce not only his claim to personal identity, but all the claims his own faith makes to be unique and different from all others. This appears to be not so much a landmark as a brick wall, an impassable obstacle which stands in the way of the meeting of minds. It is important to realise that the Hindu feels just the same, for to his way of thinking to insist on the uniqueness of Jesus, or of anyone else, is a piece of incomprehensible fanaticism which makes any intelligent conversation impossible.

But is that separate identity which Hindus feel compelled to deny, and Christians to retain, in fact the same thing? In other words, do Hindus and Christians share a common understanding of what it means to be a human being? At one level we do, for we all share in the common human experiences of birth, marriage and death; we experience anger, fear, disappointment, the joy of celebration, the pain of parting, and so on. In chapter four we shall be exploring

16

some other areas of common experience. Yet there are profound differences, of which the most important is that the Hindu social order is *hierarchical*, that is to say, it is based on an institutionalised and permanent inequality which is backed by religious sanctions. Everyone has a defined position in the social scale. So marked is this principle that the social anthropologist Louis Dumont entitled a book about Indian society *Homo Hierarchicus*— hierarchical man. Those who live by Vedanta philosophy would want to say that these differences disappear in the ultimate experience of release from the burden of rebirth. They also assume less importance in some devotional movements, but it is in the ordinary social order that most people live their lives, and it is here that the Christian meets them.

2. Hierarchy can be seen most clearly in the Hindu joint family system in which married sons and their families continue to live with their parents instead of setting up their own households. This system is now changing but its attitudes still prevail. A friend of mine, a retired lawyer of well over 80, was head of such a family for many years and once I got him to talk about it: "I was like God and my word was absolute law. It was unthinkable that anyone should challenge a decision of mine even in his thoughts. I was the arbiter in all quarrels, but when I retired I handed over my authority to my eldest son. I gave him the keys in front of all the family and said to them all: 'From this moment, he is in charge.' Next day my two sons had a quarrel and as usual came to me to sort it out, but I said nothing, so they realised that my decision was genuine." All family life was governed by strict rules. A son would not speak in the presence of his father unless spoken to and a younger brother would similarly remain silent in the presence of his elders. When visiting a Hindu home I have sometimes tried to draw out a younger member of the family in conversation and been puzzled by his reluctance. Yet outside the home he will be willing and eager to talk.

One is continually surprised at the seemingly peremptory

way in which a father will order his adult son to bring something from another part of the house, or to take a message to someone else. Often a similar relationship can be seen between, for example, senior university professors and their juniors. Once a junior lecturer said to me of his head of department, to whom he owed his appointment: "I always arrive before him and leave after him and do anything he tells me without question." That sort of behaviour might be found perhaps in a western firm or office and yet it is taken to an extreme in India which a westerner finds strange. Dominance has as its corollary dependence. A Hindu father will give his grown-up son financial help, find him a job, help him out in difficulties with his wife and children in a way which to the western mind suggests that the son has never outgrown adolescence and that the relationship between father and son has remained fixed in the pattern of childhood. Moral behaviour seems to depend on the threat of punishment, there seems to be little conception of what we would call a self-imposed moral discipline. This is particularly clear in matters of sex. Boys and girls can never be left alone together, for there is no telling what they might get up to.

Young people are content to leave the choice of a marriage partner in their parents' hands and, until recent years, would never have thought that anything else was possible. In this area of life, as in so many others, independent personal choice is as unthinkable to the Hindu as it is fundamental to the westerner.

As one would expect, Indian Christian patterns of behaviour are sometimes very similar to Hindu, and this can sometimes have strange consequences. Once I was talking with a missionary colleague of many years experience in theological education, who was also the author of several books. I asked if he was planning to do any more writing. He replied:

"I see my job as getting other people to write rather than as writing myself. Most teachers think they should not publish anything until they have got their PhD. To do so is somehow to set themselves above the college principal. But when they have got their PhD they become principals themselves and so have no time to write, and so you lose them both ways. Or else they feel they can only write something if they are specially invited to so do for a conference. No-one ever writes to the *Indian Journal of Theology* to say they disagree with some article in a previous issue. There is no published debate."

The Hindu principle of hierarchy is thus reflected in many areas of life. Similarly the Christian principle of the equal value of all men in the sight of God is reflected in many areas of western society. The distinction is not absolute for the west knows something of hierarchy, and India is being increasingly influenced by egalitarian ideas, nonetheless this distinction does point to two fundamentally different intuitions about what it means to be human.

Can we penetrate any further into the meaning of this difference? I believe that we can. Carl Jung has written:

"The development of consciousness inevitably leads not only to separation from the mother but to separation from the parents and the whole family circle and thus to a relative degree of detachment from the unconscious and the world of instinct."[1]

This process of separation, according to Jung, sets a man free to devote his energies and his loyalty to the service of his profession, to church or to city, to the institution or firm for which he works. Now in the typical Hindu joint family that separation never happens, and thus energies and loyalties remain turned inward on the family and its extension, the caste or kinship group.

This helps one to understand many other aspects of Hindu social life which are at first sight baffling. It explains the endemic factionalism which usually seems to be based on family and caste loyalties. It explains why a man in a position of influence is expected to find jobs for a wide range of relatives, regardless of their qualifications or abilities. The wife of a man who had been recently promoted once said to me: "I never knew my husband had so many relations until now."

Family relationships not only have the highest moral claim, they are also used to interpret other claims. It often seems as if there is no other model of human togetherness. The foreigner finds himself addressed as uncle or brother, and his wife as aunty or sister. A Hindu novelist has written:

"Here in India. . . relationships between people are not counted as friendships but rather as kinships. People of one's parents' generation are invariably mother, father, paternal uncle, maternal aunt and so on. He who is a contemporary becomes brother, and his wife sister-in-law."[2]

We must now move on to the third landmark, which though of a very different kind, will eventually bring us back to the same place.

3. In his daily life a man is constantly faced with a multitude of decisions, when to go on a journey, to start a legal case, or (if he is rich enough) to start building his house. To the western mind these things might seem to be matters of personal convenience but this is not so for the Hindu. For him, life is open to all manner of powerful influences and so it is vitally important to begin any new venture at an auspicious moment or else it may end in disaster. In general the two weeks of the month when the moon is waxing are auspicious, while the period when it is waning is inauspicious.

Each year a number of astrological calendars are published in Varanasi. One of them shows how the important constellations affect travelling. Some of them are beneficial in their effects, some harmful, and others neutral. Some are beneficial provided they do not fall on a day of the week which is in itself inauspicious for travelling in a certain direction. A table shows how certain objects—a piece of silver for example—can be carried or applied to the person to counteract the dangerous influence.

It is very common to see a man wearing a ring in which is set a polished semi-precious stone. These stones are believed to act in the same way as lightning conductors. A student friend of mine once told me how a friend of his had been involved in a bad car crash from which he had miraculously emerged unscathed, while the stone in his ring had been shattered to pieces. Again, if personal disaster strikes in the shape of, for example, an untimely death in the family, it is often to the astrologer that a Hindu will go for relief. He will probably be told that he has fallen under the malevolent influence of some planet, and that he should wear one of these rings to protect himself in future.

Now astrology is one of those subjects which a western Christian finds it difficult to take seriously, yet its influence is all-pervasive among Hindus and unless one can understand it sympathetically one cannot really meet them. In order to make sense of it one has to remember two facts. The first is that it is based on a pre-scientific outlook. Broadly speaking the scientific outlook sees man as living in a world of objects which are connected to each other in series which form a basis for universal and predictable laws. There is a clear chain of cause and effect which explains why the car accident happened. But for the pre-scientific Hindu mind this is not so. Man is surrounded by a multitude of unpredictable forces which may be benevolent or malign. What astrology does is to provide a 'map' of these forces, and the necessary means to use or counteract them.

Second, under the influence of modern psychology we regard our life's drama as internal, and when things go wrong we speak of such things as anxiety neuroses which we assume happen inside the mind. Hindus turn this inside out, and so trouble is explained in terms of an invasion from without.

Accordingly, while as a means of 'scientific' interpretation astrology is patent nonsense, as a means of therapy for those whose thinking is still largely pre-scientific it is most effective. This is especially true at times of acute anxiety or sickness—experience which in all cultures make a man feel isolated from his fellows. The doctor who can name my illness as malaria or hepatitis gives me the reassurance that I am not isolated, for my complaint fits into a known category. The astrologer who tells a man that his child's death was due to the influence of a certain planet offers a comparable kind of reassurance.

It is now possible to see the point on which our three landmarks converge. They all suggest that the Hindu puts much less emphasis on the independent responsible personality than does the Christian. The merging of the individual into a greater reality which absorbs him, the hierarchical social system which demands unquestioning obedience from its members who are not expected to make their own decisions, the apparent lack of any sense of obligation beyond the range of family and caste, the picture of man's daily life as being surrounded by all manner of influences which inhibit his individual action, all these things point to a way of being human which is very different from our own.

These differences pose the most searching questions for the Christian who wants to communicate with Hindus, and they have obvious implications for evangelism. At this stage, however, let us recognise that besides creating problems, such differences have a very positive function. They enable the Christian to look at his own faith with new eyes. All that we have considered in this chapter gives a new and profound significance to those familiar sentences from Genesis:

"The Lord said to Abram: 'Leave your own country, your kinsmen, and your father's house, and go to a country that I will show you. I will make you into a great nation.'" Genesis 12. 1-2)

The archetypal Hebrew is called to leave the natural world of family, and to become a new kind of man, living in perpetual tension between the promise and its unknown fulfilment. He charts his course not by reading the stars but by trusting the God who has called him. Here is the source and pattern of the Christian understanding of man. I choose, therefore I am.

Having looked at his faith with new eyes, the Christian is then in a position to have a closer look at himself. In this chapter I have sometimes described myself as a westerner and sometimes as a Christian. This is not to commit the monumental blunder of assuming that these two words really mean the same thing, it is to acknowledge the fact that when I look at Hinduism I find it very difficult to disentangle the subjective from the objective elements in my looking. For example, how far is my emphasis on the separate responsible individual Christian or merely western? It is important to go on asking this sort of question all the time, even though one can never reach a finally satisfying answer, for no man fully knows himself.

Nevertheless, I can to some extent be aware of the difference. I can recognise that while our western individualism does have some Christian antecedents it is far from adequate as a pattern for living. I can then go back to Hinduism and see what it has to offer.

In the joint family every member has his place, including the old and infirm. Hindus find the very idea of geriatric hospitals incomprehensible if not barbaric.

While western man has separated himself from the world of instinct and the unconscious, he cannot in the end live without these things. He must return to them and reclaim them in a new way. There is some evidence that we are beginning to realise this. The charismatic movement, the prayer of silence, the recovery of movement and physical contact in worship, all these things are signs of our slow and fumbling rediscovery of a part of ourselves that we had lost. This is an area where Hinduism has much to teach us.

Even so bizarre a phenemenon as astrology has something to offer, for the man who lives by astrology knows he is part of nature and part of the universe. The environmental crisis is reminding us in a painful way that we forget this at our peril.

There is another important aspect of this looking at himself that the missionary must undertake. My view not only of Hinduism but also of the obligations and opportunities which I have towards it is filtered through that history to which, quite inescapably, I am the heir. To understand my role I must therefore know something of the past.

Chapter 2

A GLANCE AT THE PAST

In the first chapter we considered the missionary as an explorer: this is not just a preliminary to other things, a first stage which can be passed through and then left behind. It is a continuing and essential part of the missionary's vocation. The man who stops exploring becomes insensitive to people and to situations, while the man who goes on is kept humble and fascinated—an attitude which is halfway to love.

But the missionary today is rarely an explorer in virgin territory. He is not, like St Paul at Athens, the first Christian to arrive on the scene. Others have been there before him. The fact of his coming puts him into a living relationship with them, they become part of his past, and whether he likes it or not he becomes an heir to their tradition. The past is still very much alive and shapes the present. The missionary therefore needs to study the history of the Christian enterprise in his area. How did his predecessors understand and set about their task? How far must he repudiate and how far should he endorse their methods and their attitudes? Further, those who came before him founded a church. Both they and it have made a certain impression. What have Hindus thought of the Christian presence among them, and how have they reacted to it? This is an important question and sometimes also a painful one, for the impression which we make on others rarely corresponds to what we intend. What Hindus have thought about the church and about its missionaries in the past will largely govern what they expect of them today. Thus while it is important to know what Christians have made of Hinduism, it is no less important to know what Hindus have made of Christianity.

Like the exploration described in Chapter One this study of the past must be a continuing process and it needs to be informed by a similar attitude of humble sensitivity. In the church today there is a growing and commendable desire to do justice to other religions, but this is not often matched by a similar approach to our own past. Unfortunately the history of the Christian mission is a subject on which all too little research has yet been done. This is particularly true of the 19th and early 20th centuries for which there is an abundance of material available in the archives of the missionary societies as well as in the areas where the missionaries actually worked. The result is that it is not yet possible to come to a realistic and reasonably objective understanding of the past.[1] Traditional descriptions usually made the foreign missionary an isolated figure. Too little was written about his national colleagues and of the local church of which they and he were members, nor was the work set in the political, social, and economic context of its time. The gap was filled by the kind of hagiography which made the missionary twice as large as life. It is hardly surprising that there is a reaction today—part of a much wider reaction against the past—and that the very word 'missionary' suggests someone who is either a dangerous fanatic or a hopeless romantic—a religious version of either Dr Goebbels or Don Quixote.

What follows makes no claim to be the result of genuine scholarly research, still less does it make any claim to remedy those defects which I have just mentioned. It is simply a brief glance at the work of a few Christians, mainly Europeans, among the educated Hindus of Varanasi in a short period in the middle of the last century. This choice was dictated by the fact that the material was readily available. If I have written little about other Christians and other periods, it is not because I underestimate their significance, but because I have not studied the subject in depth. Obviously the ideal would have been to write a continuous history of the Christian mission in Varanasi from its beginnings early in the last century down to the present day, for only against that complete background can the missionary really know what he has inherited. Yet while this chapter is sadly incomplete, it may still be sufficient to evoke awareness. A sensitive awareness of the past may be more important than a complete knowledge of it.

There was a handful of Indian Christians in Varanasi in the early years of the 19th century, but it was in about 1830 that the work really got under way with the arrival of two ordained CMS missionaries, Charles Leupolt and William Smith, who both stayed for 40 years. Others came and went, but it was these two who provided the continuity. Leupolt wrote two books[2] which give a typical account of the work of a missionary of that period in India. He devoted himself to the nurture of the young church, which meant that Smith was free to devote his time to evangelism. He wrote a book[3] in which he described the conversations he had over a period of four years with a very able Hindu scholar who was eventually baptised, taking the name of Nehemiah Goreh. Goreh himself became a prolific writer and exercised a considerable ministry in Varanasi and elsewhere. He had first come into contact with Christianity through a polemical tract in which Hinduism was attacked, and it was with the intention of refuting this that he first sought out William Smith. The tract, in fact a poem in Sanskrit couplets, was written by J. Muir, principal of the government Sanskrit College, now the Sanskrit University of Varanasi. The college had been established in 1791 with the threefold aim of demonstrating to Hindus that their new British rulers respected their religion and culture and were not bent on destroying it, of training Hindu pundits so that they could interpret their traditional law for the benefit of British judges who were to preside over the newly organised courts, and of introducing oriental learning to the West.[4] Besides Muir other members of the staff of this college combined their Sanskrit scholarship with a devotion to the missionary enterprise. Notable among them was one J. R. Ballantyne.

These men were all committed to sharing with others what

they themselves had found in Christ. This is the golden chain which binds together the missionaries of every time and place. In 1866 Smith wrote in his journal:

"I was telling the old Dashashwamedh[5] Pundit this morning that the great aim of Christ's coming was to put our living requickened spirits into communion and fellowship with the living supreme spirit."[6]

That is the heart of the matter and always has been.

But also, these men saw Christ as the lynch-pin of a fixed doctrinal system, and Christianity as a set of truths to be proclaimed. Hinduism was therefore seen as a system to be refuted. Smith wrote of the need for "able preachers of the Gospel and able refuters of the Hindu system". Of a conversation with a group of pundits he observed: "I stated some points of their doctrines and the objections I felt towards them and thus gradually opened the way for a declaration of the nature of God, the creation of man, and sin and the way of salvation according to the Christian system". And Goreh's biographer wrote of him:

"His subtle intellect was ever striving to prove by natural reasoning what he firmly held as a matter of faith."[7]

Ballantyne could quote with approval a certain John Penrose who was Bampton Lecturer in 1808 and who wrote:

"When those persons to whom our religion is offered shall be able to determine for themselves, concerning its records and evidences, they will learn its truth on rational principles."[8]

All this was bound to set a high premium on words, and especially on words used in rational argument; it was also difficult on these terms to have a positive approach to Hindu thought which remained a system to be refuted. Yet there were times when Smith at any rate felt that words were not enough. Like most missionaries of the period he devoted much of his time to 'itinerating'. In 1850 he commented:

"Flying about from town to town and village to village is not wise excepting on occasions. These people have drunk in the doctrines of their religion from their infancy in a much deeper manner, generally speaking, than

Christians have done. It is not to be expected that a passing harangue or two, a quarter of which is probably understood and one half of that misapplied, will be sufficient to affect the person."

and in 1854 he reflected that "it would be very useful if we had clear and concise accounts of the causes at work in the conversion of different nations in ancient and modern times".

One can sense that Smith was feeling after a deeper understanding of his task—something that the rudimentary tools of the nineteenth century could not provide. The modern disciplines of social anthropology and psychology now enable us to understand much better than the Victorians could the forces which mould the lives of individuals and communities. This makes us put correspondingly less weight on the effect of words used in reasoned argument. Was it because he expected too much of words that Smith was sometimes very discouraged? ". . . I feel deeply concerned that one year after another should pass without our endeavours yielding any visible fruit."

As a trained philosopher and a considerable Sanskrit scholar J. R. Ballantyne was very much preoccupied with language and with the educated Hindu:

"It is not on the ground of its intrinsic value (though I may have my own private opinion of its value), that I recommend the Hindu philosophy to the missionary among the Hindus, as a thing to be mastered, not merely dipped into. It is in order that he may be under no temptation splenetically to turn his back upon the learned of the land, and to act as if only the uneducated had souls to be saved."[9]

He could be bitingly critical of missionaries who appealed to the heart at the expense of the head—for by no means all relied on the power of reasoned argument—and who dismissed Hinduism as the wiles of Satan:

"It is perfectly idle to tell the Hindu thinker that his speculative belief is a 'delusion of Satan'. You yourself would be the first to exclaim 'pooh pooh' if a missionary *Shaman* from Siberia were to demand your allegiance to his creed, not tendering to you its justification or evidences, but relying on the rhetorical flourish that your Christianity is a wile of Satan, and yourself a stiff-necked misbeliever."[10]

He came across an article in a missionary magazine in which the writer did this very thing, attributing Hindu philosophy to delusions inspired by Satan. If this were so then of course there was no need for the missionary to study the philosophy and so try to meet the pundits on their own ground. He could simply reduce them to silence by the power of the Gospel. Ballantyne showed this article to a group of pundits and one of them commented:

"Missionaries mistake our silence. When a reply, which we think nonsense, or not applicable, is offered to us, we think that to retire silently and civilly from such useless discussion is more meritorious than to continue it. But our silence is not a sign of our admission of defeat which the missionaries think to be so. We are not averse to hearing reasons on the side of a religion which our masters hold, and we think that there will be an interest, on the attempt's being fulfilled—which you undertake— to show us, by a Sanskrit Commentary, that Christianity is not so unreasonable as it appears to be when preached without reason."[11]

Ballantyne was passionate in his defence of Hindu scholars against the attacks of missionaries, though his passion could lead him to write some tortuous prose:

"In speaking up for my friends the pundits, I have not been able to avoid—I could not with propriety have avoided—a tone that may seem defiant. A deprecatory tone—a tone 'apologetic' in the modern sense of the word—would have been unjust to the Pundit as it is undue to those who, in their ignorance, preposterously look down on him."[12]

Yet Ballantyne's quarrel was not with mission as such but with its abuse: to a missionary critic he wrote:

"In the 'contempt for missionaries' which you allude to I am no participant. I have said again and again that I would not have them relax their present efforts, but that I would not have them regard their present efforts as either the *one* thing needful in the way of *means*, or at the outset the most important. You are quite wrong therefore, when you turn upon me and ask what fruit I have to show. Why, I have been but 'digging and dunging' hitherto,—but I am going on systematically and I *can* show fruit (not in the shape of course of completed Christians) *at every stage of my course.* I have brought the Sanskrit College to be, from a place in which English was regarded as pollution to a Brahmin's throat, to be a place in which English. . . is eagerly studied by the *foremost* Brahmins—to be a place in which the men. . . are now *avowedly* ready to hear what I can advance in the shape of a '*reason* for the faith that is in me.' And you tauntingly ask me where are *my* fruits. *These* are all that I yet lay claim to. And who can gainsay them?"[13]

The kind of thing which Ballantyne criticised has too often disfigured the missionary enterprise, and its effects are still felt today, but his language must have further antagonised the very men he wanted so much to persuade. One would dearly like to know what he and Smith thought of each other. Yet his thorough grasp of Sanskrit language and philosophy, his intellectual rigour, his long-term vision of his work, and above all the fact that he could genuinely write of 'my friends the pundits'—all these are the abiding principles of any serious Christian approach to the educated men of other faiths. He is a humbling reminder of the fact that though the modern use of the word 'dialogue' is new, what it stands for is not.

He, Goreh and Smith lived in a situation of continual intellectual intercourse with Hindus, a task to which they were able to devote most of their time and energy. In one of his annual reports to CMS Smith gave a vivid picture of this activity:

31

"In respect to the nature and extent of the work—the sermons to be preached, the arguments to be held, the books to be written, the intercourse with natives to be cultivated, the prejudices and misunderstandings to be removed etc. etc, it is often very difficult even for those engaged in it to form an adequate idea or to know what duty ought to have most of our attention and how it ought to be discharged."

That is one small part of the tradition to which a missionary in Varanasi is heir.

We must now glance at the other side of the coin and ask what Hindus have made of Christians. Hindus gladly and gratefully acknowledge the great contribution made by western scholars—many of whom, like Ballantyne, were Christians—to Sanskrit studies. They also acknowledge the Christian ideal of service which they have seen embodied in the great colleges and hospitals and in countless smaller institutions as well. These have done much to spread Christian ideals and the Christian ethic in many areas of Hindu society. Yet with this there has often gone a deep suspicion of the motives of the scholarship and more particularly of the service. A history of Sanskrit literature written in Hindi and published in Varanasi in 1965 quotes from a letter said to have been written by the great Sanskrit scholar Max Muller: "The ancient religion of India is doomed and if Christianity does not step in whose fault will it be?" The author quotes from another letter said to have been addressed to Muller by one E. B. Russey: ". . . your work will form a new era in the efforts for the conversion of India". The author then adds his own comments:

"Later Western scholars copied Max Muller. The question arises, did Western scholars really expend so much labour on the Veda[14] with malicious intent? To destroy the root of Indian religion and to spread Christianity?"[15]

How far that accusation is true can only be decided by

research, but the point is, it is almost universally believed to be true by educated Hindus in this part of India. As one such man once said to me: "Of course I am glad that you are studying Sanskrit but I fear that you may only be doing so in order that in the end you can say you have proved that Hinduism is all nonsense."

It is also universally assumed that missionaries offer bribes in the shape of food, clothing and education to the poor and uneducated in order to persuade them to become Christians. Behind these suspicions and misunderstandings there lies a deep-rooted antipathy to conversion. Some words of Nehemiah Goreh remain as true today as when he wrote them a century or more ago:

> "Our countrymen look upon us, the native converts, as the most wicked of all men. They know that men do all sorts of wicked things for the sake of money, or 'belly' as they say. And so they can well believe that we have given up our religion for the sake of money. But they cannot possibly imagine that anyone can give up the sacred religion of the Vedas, and his faith, from any good motive."[16]

When one adds to this the naturally suspicious bent of the Hindu mind, of which we shall have more to say in the next chapter, then the missionary's task appears formidable indeed. In addition, while in Varanasi there seems to have been some meeting of minds in the period we have glanced at, this is no longer true today. Local Hindus are only too well aware of what Christians criticise. My first teacher at the Sanskrit University would introduce any remark on image worship, the caste system or astrology, by saying: "Of course, I know you people don't believe in it, but. . ." Yet he was wholly ignorant of anything that Christians positively affirm. Nowadays first-hand knowledge of Christian teaching is largely confined to the small minority of those who can speak and read English fluently, and most of these are to be found in the older generation.

The century that has elapsed since the days of Smith and Ballantyne saw the rise and fulfilment of the movement for Indian Independence. For the most part the church in India stood aside from this movement and so Christianity was even more closely identified with British rule in the minds of Hindus. My retired lawyer friend once told me of a conversation he had with a missionary who had asked in some frustration why so few people came to hear him preach. My friend replied: "Because you criticise Hinduism under the protection of British bayonets."

One aspect of the independence movement was a literary renaissance. Varanasi was and remains an important centre for a new kind of Hindi from which has sprung a rich crop of novels, short stories, essays and poetry. The standard history of this renaissance, itself written in Hindi, has much to say of the influence of Shelley and Keats, of de Maupassant, Marx and Freud, on the minds of the new writers, yet at no point is there any hint of the direct influence of Christ and Christianity, nor has the Indian Church provided any significant Hindi writer. For the indirect influence of the Christian ethic and of the Christian view of man there is plenty of evidence, yet the fact remains that Christian faith never seriously engaged the minds of these writers.

Why was this so? One suspects that by now the missionaries, whether national or expatriate, were busy elsewhere. The church and its maintenance demanded more of their time. Congregations needed pastoral care, there were schools and hostels to be run. Many of the older Christians of Varanasi speak with affection and gratitude of the missionaries who taught them and loved them fifty years ago. But there was a price to be paid. The church was and still is largely drawn from so-called out-caste groups which are despised by high-caste Hindus. It is a sad fact that in Varanasi the man who lives among and associates himself with such groups is not acceptable to high-caste society. Nor would the missionaries have had the time and energy to keep in regular personal contact with high-caste educated

Hindus. There were some exceptions to this general rule. One of these was a CMS missionary called J. J. Johnson. Son of a Durham miner, he became a brilliant scholar, and could deliver fluent lectures in Sanskrit without using notes. He exercised a considerable ministry among the pundits from 1879 until his death in 1918. He was an exceptional man in every way. Nevertheless the negative evidence from the field of Hindi literature, and one's own contemporary experience, suggests that at some point the Christian ministry to the educated of the city petered out.

We have glanced briefly at the missionary's inheritance. What should be his attitude towards this very ambiguous legacy? For its many positive aspects he can only be deeply and humbly grateful, but what of the negative side? Here there are two points which stand out particularly clearly.

First, the apparent withdrawal of the missionaries from regular meeting with the educated is a fact that demands a great deal of hard thinking. A missionary, like many other people, has to live in a state of perpetual tension between the urgent and the important. By definition, the urgent always calls for immediate attention. There are accounts to be kept up to date, committee meetings to attend, visitors to meet, addresses to prepare, as well as countless other essential but time-consuming tasks. The important can always be postponed—further language study, that visit to a Hindu or Muslim friend, the book which would take one into a deeper understanding of Hinduism, that public lecture which one would love to attend if only one had the time, that hour or two of reflection on what one is really there to do. When missionaries are few in number and overworked it becomes impossible to resist the tyranny of the urgent. Those responsible for making church appointments have to live in a similar tension. There are some posts which must be filled at once: that congregation needs a pastor, this school needs a teacher in an important department. It is not easy to release a man who is urgently needed elsewhere and set him free for an important experimental ministry which may yield no obvious results for many years. In the life of the church everywhere there is probably much more sheer frustration than we realise. Since coming to Varanasi I have been much struck by the number of people—by no means all of them working in India — who have said to me: "I envy you so much. I wish I could do what you are doing". The evidence of Varanasi suggests that unless the church can release more people for full time engagement with men of other faiths at the local level, very little progress will be made.

Second, the negative reaction of so many Hindus and Muslims to much of the missionary enterprise in the past makes the missionary, quite inescapably, into a symbol of much that is not his personal responsibility. This he must accept without protest. If he is a foreigner he may be the first one on whom a Hindu or Muslim can unleash his pent-up bitterness. Once, in the company of another English Christian and two Hindu friends, I was talking with an elderly Muslim scholar in front of 60 or 70 of his students: "Jesus said that if someone strikes you on one cheek you should turn the other to him as well, but that is not what you English did. You came and conquered India by force". Part of the missionary's vocation is to act as a lightning conductor for this kind of thing. Only when the anger has been released and then accepted without retaliation can a personal meeting become possible.

When a missionary returns home on leave he is a symbol in a similar though much less painful way. He may be expected to answer questions about the policy of the government of his adopted country, about the World Council of Churches, about the use or supposed misuse of funds and goods supplied by the various aid organisations.

At such moments he can remember that Jesus was also sometimes compelled to be a symbolic figure against his will. In *St Luke* 9. 51-56 we read of some Samaritan villagers who refused to welcome him, not because he was Jesus, but simply because he was a Jew 'making for Jerusalem'. The long history of bitterness between Jews and Samaritans, for which Jesus of course was in no way responsible, prevented a meeting. Yet Jesus accepted the situation and refused to 'call down fire from heaven'.

This passage is an appropriate one for the missionary's meditation. Nobody likes to be a symbol, and so many try to escape from the entail of the past. For example there are those who say that we should abandon the very word missionary because of all the misleading associations which have become attached to it. Yet this word is not only deeply rooted in the Christian tradition—it corresponds to the word 'apostle'—it has become common currency among Hindus to such an extent that in India no alternative could possibly replace it. Whatever I may call myself, Hindus will always call me a missionary. In the New Testament the word 'messiah' was similarly both indispensable and very ambiguous. Many of the overtones which had become attached to it in the course of history obscured rather than clarified the real significance of Jesus, yet instead of rejecting the word the New Testament accepts and redeems it, and in so doing helps to redeem the past which had shaped it.

Such an attitude to the negative part of his inheritance is part of the missionary's calling. The burden does not seem unduly heavy if he remembers that he himself is a forgiven sinner, and that one day he will be a very ambiguous part of someone else's past. If he is mercifully inclined to his predecessors, he can the more readily pray that the coming generation will be no less merciful to him.

All this has a very practical bearing in Varanasi where the foreigner is asked to define himself at the beginning of every conversation. Except by little boys in the streets who want to show off their few words of English, the first question he is asked is never: "What is your name?" but rather: "From what country do you come? What are you doing in India?" In other words, people's first interest is not in who one is but in what one is. To those questions I always replied that I had come from England and that I was there to study Sanskrit. This invariably met with a most favourable response, but of course it was never enough. I had to say something to identify myself as a Christian. That word itself was of no use, for every European is by definition a Christian in Hindu eyes. I therefore had no alternative but to say that I was a missionary, knowing that this word would be hopelessly misunderstood, but hoping that the thought of a missionary who was studying Sanskrit might be sufficiently unusual to spark off some more questions. But this is to anticipate the next chapter in which we shall consider the attitudes the missionary adopts and the responses he evokes.

Chapter 3

ATTITUDES AND RESPONSES

We have seen that it is important for the missionary to discover what he can about the history of the church and its mission in his area, and to discover what sort of impression it has made on Hindus. He also needs to reflect on his role, to ask himself: what am I here for, what am I trying to do? This is particularly necessary today when so much that used to be taken for granted is under challenge. A missionary can no longer follow an established pattern, he has to work out his own. This applies with special force to the man who has been released from all other tasks in order to meet men of another faith. There is no-one else who can tell him what he is supposed to be doing. When he begins his task he is likely to find that he has a lot of time on his hands. If he is wise he will not try to invent jobs in order to keep himself occupied and justify his existence. Instead he will quietly adopt a certain attitude, and then wait to see what responses he evokes. He can never predict what those responses will be, but it is they which will both define the limits and open up the possibilities of his ministry.

When I arrived in Varanasi in 1972 I enrolled as a student at the Sanskrit University. I was an object of considerable curiosity for in recent years not many Europeans have

joined this institution. Rumour spread that I was a bishop—
"He wears a bishop's hat"—a reference to the crash helmet I
wore when riding my scooter. More than that, I was an
object of suspicion, for suspicion is deeply engrained in the
Indian psyche. Nothing is what it seems to be, no-one can be
accepted at face value.

There is a particularly clear example of the suspicion
which one commonly meets to be found in the *Bhagavata
Purana*, one of the most popular devotional books of North
India:

"A certain king went hunting in the forest. Tired and
thirsty after the chase he arrived at the dwelling of a sage
whom he asked for a drink. However the sage was so deep
in meditation that he did not hear. The king immediately
thought to himself: "This man is not really meditating, he
just pretending. By keeping quiet he is deliberately trying
to insult me."Then with the end of his bow he picked up
the body of a dead snake which he saw lying nearby and
draped it round the neck of the sage. It is one of the many
fascinations of Hinduism that the scriptures and life
continually illuminate each other in this way."

It is therefore hardly surprising if the missionary's motives
are suspected—though I was rather surprised when a Hindu
friend once admitted to me that when we first met he
thought I was an agent of the CIA: "You are a misfit as a
priest, but you have all the qualities of a political agent."

When to this there is added the impressions which Hindus
in Varanasi already have of Christianity, described in the
last chapter, then it is obvious that the missionary has to
earn his passage. His first aim must be to turn curiosity into
acceptance and suspicion into trust. How can he do this?

First, he must be *there*. Perhaps this is too obvious to need
stating. In my early days at the Sanskrit University I made it
my first task simply to be seen about and known. I attended
extra seminars and functions of which there were always
plenty, for if the missionary is to achieve anything he must
first make himself part of the familiar and unnoticed
furniture of men's minds. There is no substitute for being

40

seen around in one place over a long period of time. The great Baptist missionary William Carey once remarked that nothing of value could be achieved in India except by applying the principle of concentration. He was profoundly right.

Second, the missionary must be weak. A group of Christians at a place such as the Sanskrit University would be felt as a threat in a way that is not so true of one man on his own, but there is more to weakness than this. Some years before coming to Varanasi I was warden of a boys' hostel and manager of a primary school, two posts which in Indian society inevitably gave me power and influence. I found that I could not meet Hindus and Muslims as myself but only, so to speak, as mediated through this institutional face. My status was an obstacle to friendship. Schools and hostels need to be run and this is the proper vocation of some missionaries, but the man whose calling is to penetrate to the heart of another faith must be set free from any role which hinders his real task.

Third, the missionary must be innocent of all offence. It was my rule never to say anything critical of Hinduism in front of Hindus, and only to speak of Christ and Christianity if I was asked to do so. In Varanasi this is not only courtesy but also wisdom, though I do not suggest that it should be a universal rule.

Fourth, the missionary must show that he is genuinely interested in Hinduism for its own sake and not from any ulterior motive. He has to earn the right to be trusted by showing his interest consistently over a long time. Such patience yields rich rewards for to show that one is interested in what another man holds most precious is a sure way to win his heart. Interest has as its foundation the study and grasp of language. Having spent seven years in India before coming to Varanasi I had already been able to acquire some fluency in Hindi. This proved of inestimable value, for language is far more than a means of communication. It is the expression of a people's soul, the deeply cherished sacrament of their culture, values and religion. In a strange way this is particularly true of those whose pride has been deeply hurt, as the pride of Hindus most certainly has. Moreover a grasp of language turns one's foreignness into a priceless asset. Dialogue and evangelism, and the friendship which is the basis of them both, are worth what they cost. To work at the language is to demonstrate that one is willing to pay that cost, and so the path is open to friendship—though the missionary has to wait very patiently for the day when instead of praising him for the fact that he speaks the language, people begin to listen to what he says.

This long-term study of language and religion and much else besides is absolutely indispensable for the kind of exploration I have described in chapter one. It is the best way of disarming the hostility which I have described in chapter two, but much more than these things, it is the outward and visible evidence for a certain attitude of mind and heart. This attitude can open up new and richly creative roles for the missionary in a situation which at first sight seems deadly and hopeless.

Fifth, the missionary must be empty handed. So often we go to others as givers. We have our professional training and skill, whether as doctors, nurses or agricultural workers. Things being what they are, this usually makes the foreigner more highly qualified than his Indian colleagues who often wish they could have had the same sort of opportunities. The giver is also by definition the man of action, and so to most Hindus the word missionary at its best suggests someone who is zealous, self-disciplined and devoted to his work. It is these qualities and the love which has so often transfigured them which have won Christian schools, colleges and hospitals their great reputation.

Yet these qualities become a disadvantage for the missionary who is trying to enter as deeply as he can into another faith. He is essentially a student and as such he approaches Hindus not as a giver but as a supplicant. By asking them to teach him their language and religion he affirms their being and their dignity. This is an illustration of the familiar principle that the best way to fellowship with

42

another man is very often not to offer him anything but instead to ask something of him. Why else did Jesus ask the Samaritan woman for a drink and invite himself to dinner with Zacchaeus? I shall never forget the day when I was summoned into the presence of the Vice-Chancellor of the Sanskrit University shortly after I had joined. Among other questions he asked me where I had studied in England. I replied: "Oxford." "Oxford! It is very good of you to come here and study Sanskrit." So began a new relationship.

Sixth, the missionary must learn to wait. India affords many opportunities to learn this discipline. It can sometimes take an hour or more to cash a cheque or buy a train ticket. These times of waiting are a parable. The missionary knows days and weeks when he seems to achieve absolutely nothing and experiences a sense of utter frustration and uselessness—as indeed do most other people in most other jobs. Perhaps this is something like the dark night in the life of prayer which all the great masters describe. Perhaps too this is part of the vocation of the whole church in a bewildering and perplexing age when our role is never as clear as we would like it to be.

"I said to my soul, be still, and wait without hope
For hope would be hope for the wrong thing; wait without love.
For love would be love of the wrong thing; there is yet faith
But the faith and the love and the hope are all in the waiting."[1]

This six-fold attitude of the missionary can be summed up in a phrase of Kenneth Cragg's: 'a presence willed and intended as the presence of Christ.' It is only as people begin to make their own responses to my presence that I discover what I can actually do. Let us therefore look at some of the responses which people made to my presence during my early years in Varanasi, and see where they led. Some proved barren and led nowhere, while others opened up new and hitherto unsuspected opportunities of ministry.

There are always people who want to make use of the

missionary in order to obtain gadgets from the west which are unobtainable in India. This is a painful reminder to him that whatever his lifestyle he is a perpetual symbol of an affluence to which his Hindu friends can never hope to aspire.

Other people will ask him to teach them English. Hindi is widely spoken all over North India, and is India's official national language, but for obvious historical reasons it is not an international language like French or English. This means that the man who only knows Hindi has access to a very limited range of knowledge, and so in any modern subject English is necessary for the serious student. Harsh economic realities are more important, for English is very often the passport to a good job. Yet beneath these factors there is also a deep inner malaise. Many young Indians have lost their moorings in their own culture and so have no scale of values by which to test anything new. This makes them vulnerable to the latest western fashion or idea. It is a sad paradox that though the country has been politically independent since 1947, there is now more western cultural influence—often of a very debased kind—than ever before. It is no wonder that this produces a reaction in the patriotic and devout, who want to reject the west and all its works, including the English language.

In the Gospels the ceaseless clamour of the sick at times threatened to swamp the ministry of Christ. In an Indian city today it is the ceaseless clamour of those who beg: "Teach me English", which threatens to overwhelm the missionary if he cannot say no. Is that difference symptomatic? The missionary has to handle this response with care, and often it is almost impossible to refuse with Christian courtesy, and there are times when it is right to say yes.

I was once approached by two young Buddhist teachers at the Sanskrit University with this request. One was a monk from Sri Lanka, while the other was a layman from a village way up in the Himalayas, three days walk from the Tibetan border. My wife and I each taught them for an hour once a week. I got them to talk and write about Buddhism in

English. After a few weeks they asked if we could read the Bible together and so we started to go through *St Mark's* Gospel, using *Today's English Version*, for the idiomatic language of the *New English Bible* is much too difficult for most people in this part of the world.

When we came to "The Sabbath was made for man and not man for the Sabbath", the monk was deeply impressed: "That is a revolutionary principle." He went on to say how difficult it is for a monk to keep his rule in the modern world. He is not supposed to handle money or to eat after midday. This young man therefore finds himself living in a state of perpetual tension: "No-one knows what it means to be a good Buddhist today". One sensed that he was attracted by Christ's freedom from the law.

That is the kind of conversation which one likes to report in letters home, but in our next session we came to the healing of the man with the withered hand in *St Mark* 3.1-6, with that sinister note at the end: "and they made plans against Jesus to kill him." "Why did they want to kill him? It is not wrong to heal people." I explained that Jesus was opposed by the religious leaders of his day "just as the Brahmins opposed the Lord Buddha." "But no-one wanted to kill the Lord Buddha." "Non-violence is the cardinal moral principle of Buddhism, and I thought of how much there is in the Bible and in the chequered history of the church which would appal my friend—Elijah's slaughter of the priests of Baal, the Crucifixion itself, the Crusades, the Inquisition and all the other horrors, while it is the proud boast of Buddhists that not a drop of blood has been shed in the name of their Lord.

So in this meeting both Buddhist and Christian found themselves having to ask searching questions for which there were no easy answers.

Other responses to the missionary are more casual. The traditional Sanskrit pundit is steeped in his own tradition which he finds wholly satisfying. Because Sanskrit is even less able than Hindi to give him access to other traditions he is astonishingly ignorant of them and has no particular reason to want to find out more. But occasionally he will ask a question out of casual passing interest. "Where was Christ born? In Rome?" At Christmas time: "Why do you people have so few festivals?" In Varanasi there is some kind of Hindu festival almost every week.

One of my set texts contained a lurid description of 21 hells, together with the tortures which awaited the miscreant who was sent there. The pundit who was taking me through this text commented: "Hooker Sahib, this is nothing. You should read the description of the hells in the *Garuda Purana*. That will really make your hair stand on end. But tell me, do you have hells like this in your religion? "And then, on his way to the door to spit out some betel nut he had been chewing: "What do you people believe about eternal life?"

Then there are requests to take part in public functions. A Jain friend asked me to deliver a speech in Hindi at a function attended by three Members of Parliament on 'The Uprooting of Colonialism and Imperialism'. I spoke of the inner urge in the heart to dominate others and how it was this which must be rooted out.

A few years ago there was an earthquake in Tibet in which a number of people were killed. There are many Tibetan monks in Varanasi and so a condolence meeting was held at the Sanskrit University and representatives of the different religions were invited to recite appropriate passages from their scriptures. I was asked to recite something from the Bible, an invitation which I was delighted to receive, for it was an indication of an increasing measure of acceptance at the University.

Proceedings began with the deep-throated chanting of about 30 Tibetan monks, their Mongolian features as worn and rugged as the mountains they came from, and yet showing that gentleness which is always present in Buddhism. They were followed by a group of monks from Thailand, slightly built, their faces like so many of those faces of the Buddha that one sees in the art of South-East Asia. Then four Brahmin priests chanted part of the Veda in

Sanskrit, the gestures of their hands and fingers exactly matching the rhythm of their voices. For hundreds of years, long before they were ever committed to writing, the Vedas were handed down in this way. These men are the latest representatives of a continuous tradition going back for at least 28 centuries. Last of all I went on the platform and, feeling rather like an after-thought, read my piece from the Hindi translation of the New Testament.

Afterwards one of the pundits came up to me and said: "Why didn't you recite a *mantra*[2] in English?"

"It is our custom to read the Bible in a language the hearers can understand—and in any case English is not the original language of the Bible."

"What language did Jesus speak?"

"Aramaic."

"Not English?" Then (with a twinkle in his eye), "You should compose a *mantra* in Aramaic."

"But then the listeners couldn't understand even if I could speak it."

"Never mind, they would understand the feeling."

This incident reveals a profound difference in attitudes to language. The Christian longs above all to communicate and this involves translation. His words are of no value unless they are understood. Yet one's Hindu and Buddhist friends seem unperturbed at the absence of intellectual grasp. This can and often does lead to a mindless repetition of sacred formulae which the rising generation passes by with a yawn. Yet does not our Christian eagerness to communicate often betray the very aim it serves? The really important things can never be said directly. Why else did Christ teach in parables?

So here was another example of India's inexhaustible capacity to spring surprises on the unsuspecting Christian, and in doing so to open up a new and hitherto unsuspected range of questions. Very often it is precisely the most casual responses to his presence which reveal to the missionary whole new dimensions in the endlessly fascinating task of

47

understanding and interpretation.

Other responses are of a more personal kind. One of my fellow students was a young man from the West Indies. Three or four generations back his family emigrated there as indentured labourers to work on the sugar plantations. They have greatly prospered, but the community sense that they are losing their hold on their tradition, so they have sent this young man to Varanasi to study Sanskrit. He has come back to the source, and hopes eventually to return to the West Indies and pass on what he has learnt. One day, after our class was over, he said to me: "I want to ask you something. How do you think I should set about my work when I go back? Should I concentrate on one place or travel about teaching?" I replied: "I think that to begin with you should concentrate on one place. When your work has taken root there, you can afford to spread out a bit, but you cannot do anything unless you first put down roots." Since that conversation he has asked me to lend him books on church organisation and these have given him some practical ideas.

Another friend is a scholar in Hindi. He has written several books, the most recent being a dictionary of Hindi idioms. Before this was actually published he showed me his first draft of the introduction. In this he had made some critical remarks about another writer who had produced a similar dictionary. I commented on this and he asked: "Do you think I should have written it?" "Yes, you are not making a personal attack on the author, but criticising his work. Your concern is for the development and improvement of Hindi and so it is your duty to criticise second-rate work."

The West Indian student was uncertain about the demands of his vocation, and the Hindi scholar about the demands of his integrity. The very fact that these questions were asked revealed a measure of trust, for each was the kind of question in which a man to some extent makes himself vulnerable. To receive such trust is a privilege which the missionary has to earn, it is never a right he can assume. His first task is not to break the bruised reed or snuff out the smouldering wick, but to help such men to discover the path of their vocation and their integrity—while remembering that he himself often stands in need of similar assistance from others. The missionary therefore must answer questions like this in the spirit in which they are asked. This means that he will not at this point speak directly *about* Christ, but rather *from* him, trying to show those qualities of gentleness and approachability which are the foundation of any pastoral ministry, and appealing to what is good and lovely and honest in the heart and mind of the questioner. Such an attitude enables a friendship to grow. This is not of course the missionary's final goal, but it is only by this path that the goal will be reached in the end, and there are no short cuts. At moments such as this he can do a lot worse than ponder on that long record of the endless patience of God which we call the Old Testament. This is a reminder to him that the divine urgency is not to be confused with his own impatience, and that one form of unbelief may be to attempt a thing before its proper time.

After I had been at the Sanskrit University for about two years I was asked to give a lecture in Hindi on the origins and development of Christianity. This was one of a series of four lectures on successive days on various aspects of religion in the modern world. The other three speakers were Hindu scholars. My lecture was well-attended, though the more orthodox Hindus were conspicuous by their absence. The response was most friendly, but this was partly due to the fact that I was a foreigner speaking in Hindi. Several people afterwards told me that they had known nothing previously about Christianity and so had valued the opportunity to learn something. There were some questions, of which one was: "Did the division between Catholic and Protestant take place before or after the coming of Christ?" It is a wry thought that those who know nothing else about us always seem to know of our divisions.

Just as the two questions I described earlier marked new stages in the growth of two personal friendships, so this occasion marked a large step forward in winning the confidence and trust of a group. After this I felt a new warmth and relaxation in my relations with individual members of the group.

A year later there came another request to speak, this time to a group of scholars, on the Christian understanding of creation. This was to be part of a series in which the other speakers were to be representatives of the different schools of Indian philosophy. The meeting was attended by about 30 people. Three or four of these were more liberal-minded pundits from the Sanskrit University, while most of the others were lecturers in modern subjects, such as economics, history or sociology, from another university in the city.

I was looking forward to hearing the other lectures in the series, but after mine nothing happened for about six months. One day I was talking with a member of the committee which had planned the series and asked why no more had taken place. He told me that the convener had some domestic problems and so was unable to do anything. On the spur of the moment I offered to be the convener and my offer was warmly accepted. As I knew it would, this involved me in some extra work, finding speakers, arranging venues, writing out and delivering invitation cards, but this was very worthwhile, for it gave me a reason to visit these men in their homes and so afforded me an *entrée* into a whole new area of Varanasi society.

So I was able to listen to Hindu scholars giving lectures and having discussions on their own philosophy. This proved a fascinating exercise, even though when the language became technical and the speakers animated, one often lost the thread. On these occasions I invariably kept quiet and only spoke at the end if invited to do so. In such circles as these it does no harm whatever for the Christian to be known as one who prefers listening to speaking. This also means that when he does speak he is much more likely to command a hearing. Most of these men have one foot in their own tradition and one in the 20th century, and are perplexed as to how to relate the two. This is a perplexity in which Christians share, so here was a context in which it was possible to speak as one who shared a common problem, rather than as one who thought he knew all the answers.

This group did not limit itself to discussing creation, and on one occasion there was a seminar on religion and change. I was asked to introduce this by speaking about the situation in the west. One of the group, who edits a Hindi magazine, asked me to expand my remarks into an article. I did so and was later asked to write again on any subject I liked. So a whole new area of witness and ministry opened up, albeit of a rather indirect kind.

This is a brief selection from the wide range of responses that one's presence evoked over a period of six years. They were deeply satisfying and encouraging, for to be affirmed and accepted by others in this way is an elemental human need. The missionary, like anyone else, needs to find a role in which he can gladly and freely give himself, and in which he can be genuinely creative. His role is not defined by his training and skills, for he is not so much a professional worker as an artist. An artist is a man who is consumed by a vision which he longs to express, but in order to do this he must have a thorough and practical knowledge of his medium. Wood, stone, music and paint are all different media, each with its own very different possibilities and limitations. The artist who tries to force his vision onto his material in a way which is alien to the latter will destroy both the material and the vision and maybe himself as well. So too the missionary must understand the possibilities of his own time and place and work within them, for they are the medium in which his vision must be embodied. The responses he evokes teach him what those possibilities and limitations are, while the model for his faltering and clumsy hands is that divine masterpiece which we call the Incarnation. Christ by his art turned fishermen into disciples and then into friends, and so the missionary must submit himself to the disciplines of friendship.

Chapter 4

THE PARADOX OF FRIENDSHIP

What is friendship? To define it is impossible, for it is as rich and many-sided as life itself. Its flavour and its possibilities are caught in some words of T. R. Glover:

"The Gospel began with friendship, and we know from common life what that is, and how it works. In this easier and more careless intercourse, when the mind is off guard, it is receiving a host of unnoticed impressions, which in the long run may have extraordinary influence. Pleasant and easy-going, a perpetual source of interest and rest of mind, the friendship continues, till we find to our surprise that we are changed. Stage by stage, as one comes to know one's friend, one lives the other man's life, sees and feels things as he does, and wakes up to find oneself, as it were, remade by the other's personality."[1]

This sort of human intercourse bears a family likeness to what Christians mean by prayer, which has as its goal the largely unconscious fashioning of the person who prays into the likeness of Christ. In a similar way, to be a member of a community also has a transforming effect. We all know the typical colonel, trade union official, or Anglican clergyman, all of whom have been unconsciously shaped by the influence and tradition of the group to which they belong.

But what happens when the friendship takes place across the frontiers of religion? Does not the Christian put himself in a position of some risk? Indeed he does, for taking risks is part of our vocation. We are not meant to bury our talent in the earth, nor in our unbelief to put out our hand to steady the ark of God when it looks like falling. The process Glover describes is, being unconscious, quite inescapable. The Christian who, from timidity, tries to close himself up against the other man, destroys the link between them, for friendship can only be an open door through which the traffic passes in both directions.

Yet while we must accept its risks we must not claim for friendship more than it can achieve, it cannot automatically make a Hindu into a Christian or a Christian into a Hindu, and to believe that it can is to forget the importance of conscious and deliberate choice. It is also grossly to overrate the possibilities of the relationship, for both Hindu and Christian are moulded by their own community and tradition to an extent which makes the links between them tenuous and fragile as gossamer. Such friendship is a paradox; to enter it is to experience both nearness and distance at the same time, and each somehow enhances the other. In the first chapter we glanced briefly at a small area of Hindu thought and assumption, while in the second we looked at the entail of the past in Varanasi. These influences, and many others besides them, form the unconscious background to every conversation. The result is that our traditional Christian language is, to a Hindu, not only unintelligible, but also offensive. We have already seen his profound antipathy to the very idea of conversion, and to the Christian insistence on the distinctiveness of Jesus. In addition, salvation for a Hindu involves release from the wearisome round of rebirths into this ephemeral world. He is happy to concede that devotion to Christ is an aid to the attainment of this state, but so too is devotion to Krishna or Muhammad. To tell him he must be born again is not good news but bad, while to tell him he is a sinner is to invite his contempt. As a puzzled man once said to me: "Sin and guilt have imposed a terrible burden on man. Why do you Christians make him a sinner who has to run to God to escape from his sin like someone being chased by a dog?"

We are therefore driven to the painful and forbidding conclusion that at the intellectual level meeting is extraordinarily difficult, a situation which is evoked in all its bitterness and poignancy in Roy Fuller's poem, *Spring 1942*:

Once as we were sitting by
The falling sun, the thickening air,
The Chaplain came against the sky
And quietly took a vacant chair.

And under the tobacco smoke:
'Freedom' he said, and 'Good' and 'Duty.'
We stared as though a savage spoke.
The scene took on a singular beauty.

And we made no reply to that
Obscure, remote communication,
But only looked out where the flat
Meadow dissolved in vegetation.

And thought: O sick, insatiable
And constant lust; O death, our future;
O revolution in the whole
Of human use of man and nature![2]

Yet in spite of all that and even in the midst of it, the responses which I described in the last chapter can lead to rewarding and creative encounters at other levels. This is the other side of the paradox, and for the rest of this chapter we shall be looking at some examples of it.

One of my dearest friends in Varanasi was a pundit at the Sanskrit University to whose patient and gentle teaching I owe such knowledge of Hindu philosophy as I possess. He always greeted me with a warm smile, and we visited each other's homes. Like the traditionalist he was, he thought only and always in his own categories into which he easily and painlessly inserted any new information. Once he was explaining to me the significance of some of the holidays at the Sanskrit University—their number was frustratingly large: "If the teacher instructs on the eighth day of either of the lunar fortnights, he incurs sin. If the student studies on the first day, his knowledge is destroyed. Why do you people keep Sunday as your holiday?" I said that it was because on this day Jesus rose from the dead. "It's better to say he slept, then he awoke and showed his *lila* (divine sport)." So in a few casual sentences Christ is transformed into a Hindu deity. Yet the gulf dividing our minds does not prevent the meeting of hearts.

In the last chapter I mentioned the Buddhist who lives near the Tibetan border. Once I asked him how he first came to study Buddhist philosophy:

"My father was a *lama*. He used to perform the rituals but when I asked him what they meant he could not explain them. Then a doctor returned to our village after studying for many years in Tibet. He taught me the Tibetan script and grammar. Then I came to Varanasi and found a Tibetan monk to teach me."

His home village seems to be part of a disintegrating society for since 1959 it has been cut off from its religious and cultural roots in Tibet. Many have taken to drink, while others have gone off to seek their fortune in the big cities of the plains of India—a sadly ironic contrast to the vision of Shangri-La. The younger generation are no longer interested in the Buddhist tradition, so this young man is planning to start a school where among other things that tradition can be taught:

"I held a meeting in the village and many people promised to help, but when it comes to the point they say they are too busy. I have raised about fourteen thousand rupees for the school but people in the village are still not sure that it will succeed. It is very difficult."

He is trying to retrieve and preserve what he values most deeply in the face of widespread indifference and increasing moral chaos, a situation which is familiar enough to western Christians today. So here too, in spite of the fact that as yet each of us was only a novice in the other's class, we shared a common pain and a common perplexity which enabled us to meet.

Other kinds of meeting have a more positive foundation. *Sannyasis* are a common sight in Varanasi. Their saffron robes stand out in any crowd. Broadly speaking, these men are the monks of Hinduism. They have renounced the ties of home and family in order to pursue that ultimate experience which is the goal of Vedanta philosophy. Many of the younger ones serve a kind of novitiate by studying this philosophy in one of the many small Sanskrit schools which abound in Varanasi, and which are affiliated to the much larger Sanskrit University. Not all of them have such high motives and some are downright frauds, but in studying another religion the golden rule is to look for the best. This enables one to see the worst in proper perspective.

I first met one of these young men at a meeting of Hindus and Christians arranged by the local Roman Catholics. Later I went to see him in the hostel where he lives. This was the beginning of a most stimulating friendship. Eventually I felt I could ask him how he had become a *sannyasi*. This is a question one has to approach with tact, for so complete is the renunciation expected of these men that they often regard it as wrong to speak of the past at all. My friend said:

"I come from a high-caste Brahmin family. My parents are both very orthodox and devout. My father still practises *yoga* at home and when I was a child my mother told me many many beautiful Hindu stories. They wanted me to become an engineer, but I wanted to be a *sannyasi*, so I became an army officer as the next best thing. Like a *sannyasi* an army officer is supposed to think not of himself but of others. An officer has his superiors behind him and has to go wherever they send him. A *sannyasi* has God behind him and has to go wherever God sends him. Also I must have had good *sanskaras*[3] from my previous birth.

"I remember the first time my mother met me after I had become a *sannyasi*; we met by the river Ganges here in Varanasi. She told me that when she was expecting me she had a dream that her child would become a great man. This meeting reminded her of the dream. I was so glad when she told me this, for I knew that I had her support, and this made me want to become a better *sannyasi*."

A few days before this conversation I had been reading one of the great Sanskrit classics, Ashwaghosh's *Life of the Buddha*. This poem describes how when the mother of the future Buddha was pregnant she too had a dream. A white elephant, symbol of royalty, entered her womb, and so she knew that her son would be a great man. So here is another pattern of Annunciation.

Here too, in spite of the intellectual barriers to communication, it proved possible to meet this *sannyasi* at the level of a common humanity, in this case of commitment. When he had told me of his mother I was prompted to tell him of the letter my father had written to me, assuring me of his support and his prayers, just before I sailed for India as a missionary for the first time, in 1965.

There are other experiences which are common to all traditions and which thus afford a way of meeting. One of these is personal transformation. For while, as we have seen, Hindus reject the notion of conversion from one religion to another it is not uncommon, especially today, for a man to give up his tradition and then, so to speak, be converted back to it in a rather different form. Sometimes this seems to release in the convert new springs of creativity which are not found in the man who has never left home.

I first met one such man on his initiative. He had heard about me through a mutual acquaintance and asked me to correct the English of a book he was writing, an English translation and commentary on an important Hindu text. Anything which can contribute to inter-religious understanding deserves a missionary's support and so I gladly agreed to help him.

In his younger days he was deeply involved in public life, having been at different times a lawyer, a judge and a journalist. For 14 years he was a Marxist. "A series of events bringing total disillusionment with all ideological and belief systems convinced me that all activity born of such systems of thought was useless," and he was driven back to his roots. At the age of 53 he put himself under a scholar who taught him the Sanskrit language and Hindu philosophy for seven years. Now he is a widely respected scholar and has written many books, mostly in his mother tongue, Marathi, a language of western India. He is nearer 80 than 70, but he still has a vigorous and razor-sharp mind. I owe him an immense debt for all that he has taught me about Hindu thought and experience.

To turn to religion in the second half of life is typically Hindu, but the change is not often as dramatic and as radical as his. His approach is very different from the conservative scholasticism of the Sanskrit University. I once discussed this with him. We agreed that the man who has left his tradition and then returned to it can often see it through new eyes, but he pointed out that every tradition also needs its pundits who preserve it and hand it on to the next generation even if they can do nothing else. This set me thinking of the story of the Magi. The priests in Jerusalem can tell them where Christ is to be born, but nothing else. Yet without that vital piece of information the quest of the Magi would have remained unfulfilled. My friend told me that in all his writings on Hindu texts he never ignores the traditional commentators. He reads them, absorbs them and only then can produce his own interpretation which is often very different from theirs.

This conversation helped me to look with new sympathy at the repetitious conservatism of the Church of North India—which is so like the church in many other places. It cannot interpret but can only repeat what it has, but as W. H. Auden has written:

"The function of the Church as an institution is not to convert—conversion is the work not of men but of the Holy Spirit—but to make conversion possible by continuing to preach its good news in words and liturgical acts. She must go on repeating herself, no matter whether

her repetition be passionate or, when faith is low, lifeless and mechanical, to preserve that possibility."[4]

Sometimes in North India it seems that the lamp of faith burns very low indeed, and yet the tiny church still maintains its vital work of repetition.

Not all men who have abandoned the faith of their childhood find that they can return to it with integrity, even in a different form. Once at a public lecture in the Sanskrit University I found myself sitting next to one such man who struck up a conversation. He gave me his address and since then I have many times visited him in his home. He is in his early fifties and his story is typical of many:

"As a young man I had no time for religion because I saw that what was preached was not practised. I was much influenced by socialism, by Marxism even, and later by the thought of Gandhi-ji. I and the group to which I belonged wanted to build a new society. Our life had an aim and a purpose to which we dedicated ourselves. But then I began to see that all this was Utopian. In societies where socialism is practised there is still violence, corruption and poverty. I began to feel that in the vast immensities of the universe, in time and space, life had no meaning and man can have no significance. Such meaning as he finds in the world is the product of his own mind. Perhaps it is better to be the kind of man who is content with getting and spending, with power and prestige, and not be bothered with these questions."

Yet behind his scepticism he is feeling his way back to some kind of religious view of life:

"We should reject those parts of the Hindu scriptures which merely speculate about the origins of the universe, and make use of those parts which give moral guidance, but even this is not easy for there is much in the old myths that is immoral. For example, one of the heroes of the *Mahabharat*[5] war drinks the blood of his brother; that sort of thing we cannot accept."

Do not many Christians, or people who perhaps would like to be able to call themselves Christians, feel a similar embarrassment at parts of the Old Testament?

This man works for a local research institute and shows an unusual sensitivity towards other religious communities. He once asked me how Christians feel about the use of images: "Neither Buddhists nor Jains believe in God, but they would never feel anything wrong in joining in the worship of Saraswati (the Hindu goddess of learning) at some public function, but I do not think Christians or Muslims would like to do that." I tried to explain to him the roots of our Christian antipathy to image worship. At a later meeting I asked him what he felt about conversion—as we have already seen, Hindus feel about this as strongly as Christians do about images. He replied: "India has a unique record of tolerance; each group is allowed to practise its own religion and keep its own temples in peace. Christian priests are respected as men of religion. All religions are old; conversion from one to another does not solve anything, it merely increases bitterness."

Here is a man with whom one can discuss some of the most sensitive issues which divide religious communites in India. Perhaps it is because we are both somewhat detached that we are able to do this. As a foreigner I can never fully understand what it feels like to be a member of the tiny Indian church, while my friend's personal experience has inevitably given him a certain detachment. He once told me that his Marxist principles—some of which he still retains—will not allow him to join with his neighbours in celebrating the many festivals which do so much to unify Hindu society.

These days an increasing number of people renounce their traditional faith, or a large part of it, but have no desire to return. One such is the elderly lawyer to whom I have already referred several times. I first met him when he accosted me in the street and invited me to his home. Like many of his generation he has a wide knowledge of English literature and speaks the language as well as any Englishman. There are not many Indians with whom he can share these interests and so he was delighted to meet me.

It is important for the missionary to have a few old people

among his friends. They are always ready to talk about the past and this gives a vital new perspective to all that one is learning from others. Moreover to give a little of one's time to the old now and again is a very easy and often very rewarding element of any Christian ministry.

This man had no time for organised religion in any form. As a boy he went to a local Christian school and still remembered the missionary principal who would beat little boys with the edge of a ruler until they cried with pain. Perhaps this man suffered from that feeling of insecurity which so many foreigners who have had authority over Indians have felt. Whatever the cause of his behaviour my friend never forgot it, and as a practising lawyer would always plead free of charge on behalf of any child who had suffered at the hands of a teacher. The priests of one of the leading temples in the city employed him as their lawyer. He has not a single good word for these men. He is critical of the kind of society Hinduism and Islam have produced:

"There is much sexual repression in Hinduism—just as there is among Christians—and this led to the erotic cult of Krishna. Islam bans the use of alcohol and so 90% of Urdu poetry is about it."

He often criticises the Christian attitude to Christ:

"You will never admit that he could have done wrong, yet when he cried out: 'My God, why hast thou forsaken me?' wasn't that a sign of ordinary human weakness? And why did he say to the woman taken in adultery: 'Go and sin no more'? Why didn't he even ask her what had happened? She had probably been compelled to make an unhappy marriage and was in an intolerable position. That's not sin. When I was a practising lawyer several women like that came to ask for my help."

Yet with all this he still accepts the Hindu doctrine of *karma* and rebirth which he finds the most satisfying interpretation of human life, and he cannot understand why I reject it. He knows and loves the Upanishads, the Gita and Sanskrit literature and often shows the typical Hindu antipathy to conversion: "Muslims did it at the point of the sword. You

people are more subtle; you offer bribes and inducements."
But behind this there is a passionate and practical human
concern. As a practising lawyer he was sometimes asked by
Muslims to plead on their behalf in cases involving Hindus.
They knew he would not be biassed in favour of his own
community. When he was a young man he one day saw a
child widow of the family happily playing hide and seek with
her friends:

> "She was quite unaware of the terrible fate in store for
> her. Her very shadow would be regarded as inauspicious
> and so on any important family occasion she would be
> locked in a room by herself. When she grew up her head
> would be kept shaved to prevent her from being an object
> of temptation to men."

So he decided to get this girl remarried—something unheard
of in those days over 50 years ago. After a long and difficult
battle he succeeded. He was expelled from his caste as a
result, but later got himself readmitted.

With many of his criticisms of traditional religion I could
only agree, and this amazed him: "You are a priest and you
agree with me! If I said any of these things to my own priests
they would stop their ears in fury." And of course I could
share his human concern which indeed seemed not far
removed from the intercession of the Liturgy of the Church
of North India where we pray "for justice and peace in the
whole world and for fulness of life for every man." But this is
a suggestion he will not tolerate: "Why do you always want
to drag God and religion into it? I have always been a
nonconformist and that is due to the effect of my previous
births, that is all."

To talk with with this man is always invigorating, never
dull, and often a joy, for behind all the protest there is a deep
and attractive integrity.

Such then is the paradox of friendship. But where can
friendship lead? And how does it look when we set it in the
context of some of the questions which the Christian mind is
asking today?

Chapter 5

SOME QUESTIONS

In this final chapter we must stand back a little from Varanasi in order to consider four questions which bear directly on our theme: first, what is the relationship between a local ministry such as I have described in these pages and the wider debate about other faiths which is being conducted in the church at large? This question defines the context of the other three: what is the relationship between dialogue and evangelism? What is salvation and how is it related to the spiritual experience of other faiths? How are we to assess the value and significance of our work?

Part of the missionary's role is to be a mediator between the local and the universal. The more deeply involved he becomes in his own local situation, the more necessary is it for him continually to relate this situation to the general discussion about other faiths which is being conducted through books, journals and conference reports. There is a tension here: the debate can sometimes seem very far removed from reality and is much preoccupied with the definition of abstract terms—truth claims, evangelism, dialogue, development. To some degree this is necessary. Like the common prayer of a church service and for precisely the same reasons, a general discussion has to use general terms whose meanings are broadly acceptable to all taking part, otherwise no discussion is possible; but inevitably these general terms are never adequate to describe the rich complexity of life in a particular place.

This means that the missionary has a two-fold obligation: on the one hand he must listen to what the general debate has to say to him. Others who are working in the same field have much to teach him, not least when what they say and write challenges his own assumptions. They may be able to open up for him new areas of perception and obedience to which he has hitherto been blind. Further, he must be able to justify himself to the church as a whole. His ministry must be one that others accept as valid. He must walk a razor's edge between making exaggerated claims of a spurious kind of success, and despairing of achieving anything at all. On the other hand he must address his own questions and challenges to others who are taking part in the general debate. How serious is the inadequacy of its general terms? Are the special features of his own situation, which the debate does not comprehend, of merely local interest to himself, or do they perhaps point to something of wider significance which the debate is neglecting?

This perpetual tension between the local and the universal is both necessary and creative. It is in the nature of the case that there can be no final answers to the issues it raises, but it is this tension alone which can keep one's thoughts moving in the right direction.

With all this in mind, let us look at the situation in Varanasi in the light of our second main question: what is the relationship between dialogue and evangelism?

Not much happens in Varanasi in the way of direct and organised evangelism. There is an occasional convention in one or other of the local churches, or now and then a week of tract distribution, usually conducted by outsiders who only stay for a short time, and one must not forget the hidden and unsung witness of scattered Christian families and individuals. There are also four church schools and some notable examples of Christian service. In the few years since their home for the destitute was opened by Mother Teresa, the Sisters of Charity have made a considerable and favourable impact on local Hindu opinion, but it is their rule, and a perfectly valid one, not to engage in direct preaching or evangelism.

Dialogue in its current Christian sense is a word of which very few Hindus in Varanasi have ever heard—except perhaps for a few English-speaking university professors. In other parts of India Hindu responses to Christian suggestions that dialogue might be a useful exercise have been very mixed. Some suspect it as yet another disguised attempt at conversion, while others regard it as encouraging evidence that Christians are at last coming to recognise the elementary truth that "all religions say the same thing."

Nevertheless progress is being made. The Dialogue Commission of the Roman Catholic Bishops' Conference has a dialogue secretary who has spent the last four years travelling to all parts of the country and arranging for groups of Hindus Christians and others to meet together, sometimes for several days at a time. These groups quickly discovered that to discuss doctrines led merely to barren and lengthy sermonising, they therefore limit themselves to the sharing of experience in an atmosphere of prayer and devotion. Hindu teachers in Christian schools have spoken of their fears of attempts being made to convert them, others have described their loss and rediscovery of faith—often through the teaching of Gandhi-ji. I myself took part in a meeting of Christians with Tibetan Buddhist monks, held in their temple, in which we shared our experiences of suffering.

Here is a point where the local and the universal can endorse and illuminate one another, for this corresponds very closely to the personal meetings and friendships which I have described in Chapters Three and Four. When the man in a local situation finds that his own limited experience is similar to that of others elsewhere, this gives him the confidence to believe that he really is moving in the right direction. As we have already seen, it is this kind of patient, personal meeting which slowly breaks down the prejudices of both sides and builds bridges of trust. The long term aim of the Christian in this enterprise must be to understand Hinduism and Hindus as deeply and sympathetically as he can, 'looking for landmarks' all the time, and to make Christ and Christianity in the words of J. H. Oldham, 'visible, desirable and intelligible.' As I tried to fulfil this ministry in Varanasi, I often found myself asking: is this dialogue or evangelism? More often than not I could give no clear answer to that question. Dialogue is normally assumed to be a planned and organised activity involving a group of people. Evangelism too is often, though not always, taken to be a similar kind of enterprise as the familiar phrase 'evangelistic campaign' suggests. Yet the very essence of my own ministry was that it was unorganised, unplanned, and was a continuing presence rather than an occasional activity. It cannot be fitted into the pattern of the general debate yet it did have much in common with the traditional pastoral ministry of a parish priest. This ministry has always been based on the mutual trust established between priest and people over a long time. It has always included both dialogue and evangelism but neither of these words can fully describe it. We need to add to them some such term as continual presence or personal presence. In inter-religious relationships, where trust is so vital and yet so precarious, it is this personal dimension which is of paramount importance. It needs to be brought into the centre of our contemporary discussion.

Yet even with this addition our general terms still remain very rough and ready, as the following examples show. In Varanasi there were, broadly speaking, three groups of people with whom it proved possible to establish the very varied kinds of relationship which I have described.

First, there were the orthodox traditionalists. As we have already seen, they are not usually interested in Christianity in anything more than a casual or passing fashion, yet it was through them that one was able to learn most about Hinduism. This kind of meeting can often set off the kind of internal dialogue in the mind of the missionary or of the church which I have sketched at the end of Chapter One. This is a most valuable, indeed indispensable activity. We might perhaps call it a dialogue about Hinduism, but it is patently not the same thing as a dialogue with Hindus. This is an important distinction which is obscured by the blanket use of the word dialogue.

Second, there are those who, perhaps from mere curiosity, do want to learn more about what we have to say. We have already seen how very little is actually known about Christian teaching outside the narrow circle of those who speak English. Over the years a considerable effort has been made to produce theological text books in Hindi and other Indian languages for ordinands. This is an important task and is one with which I was personally associated, yet inevitably and rightly these books assume that the reader is familiar with the main doctrines of his own faith. There is very little that one can confidently put into the hands of a thoughtful Hindu who knows nothing about Christianity but wants to learn. Here the missionary has an important function as one who can provide information in terms which can be easily grasped. This is by no means easy, for more often than not the words are simply not there. For example in Hindi the nearest one can get to 'personal relationship' is 'individual connection'. We do not realise how foreign we are. It is surely premature to talk of either dialogue or evangelism before we have learnt to say what we mean.

Third, there are those who are asking searching questions about the meaning of man, about the kind of human society we want today, and about the resources which their own tradition can provide to help in this quest. Several such men are to be found in the discussion group which I have described in Chapter Three. Here there is a paradox: while they would reject the traditional exposition of Christianity with its emphasis on the salvation of the individual in the world to come, their search for human values in the here and now, and their growing recognition of the value of change all point in a Christian direction. From a Christian point of view one could claim that Christ is the form of the future for which they are groping. But I owe it to them to point out they would all deny this interpretation and would, I think, assert that all that they are looking for is already implicit in their own tradition. Time alone will show which of us is right, but meanwhile here is an opportunity for a Christian presence of patience and love, a presence which neither the word dialogue nor the word evangelism can adequately describe.

That brings us to our third main question: what is salvation, and is it to be found in other religions? In the past, the common view of Christians was that apart from conscious surrender to Christ there could be no salvation for any man. Those who did not make that response would therefore perish, and God was not to be found in other religions. *Extra ecclesia nulla salus*: outside the church no salvation. This made the proclamation of the gospel an urgent necessity. It was a view that did full justice to certain fundamental Christian insights, the eternal significance of our choice for or against Christ, the need and the right of every man to hear the gospel, and the obligation of every Christian to spread it. However, this view did much less than justice to another and no less fundamental Christian insight, the love of God for all his creation. If a considerable portion of the human race, having had the misfortune to have been born in the wrong place or at the wrong time, was to be condemned for failing to respond to a message which it had never had the opportunity of hearing, then what became of the love of God which the message was supposedly about? Can we really worship as universal Lord a God whose writ only runs among Christians? All down the ages has he merely ignored all other men?

In India a long and distinguished line of Christian thinkers, national and foreign, have been grappling with these questions for a hundred years or more. So too in Britain have some members of that minority which has always supported and taken an active interest in the missionary enterprise. However it is only very recently—and

68

one must add very belatedly—that the church at large has started to take other religions seriously. This has coincided with a widespread malaise and loss of confidence about our present and future, and a corresponding embarrassment about our imperialist past. It is not surprising therefore that there are influential voices raised today to say that though Christ is undoubtedly the bearer of salvation for Christians he is not for other men, who can all find salvation through their own traditions. It follows that mission and evangelism are at best unnecessary and at worst immoral; for our proper task is not to try to convert others but instead to try and help them to become better Hindus, Muslims or Buddhists. More positively, our age is acutely aware of the havoc which quarrels about religion have wrought in the past and continue to cause today. Surely, if we can abandon those beliefs which separate us from other men it will be much easier for us all to meet and work together to create that better world for which all men long so desparately.

Perhaps because it corresponds so closely to the contemporary mood this view is attractive to many, but on closer examination it breaks down for two reasons. *First*, there is a considerable body of men and women, not least in India, who tell us that what they have found in Christ is wholly new and unprecedented. Once I asked a recent convert what in particular had drawn him to Christ. He replied: "The kind of love which asks no questions about the qualifications of the recipient: that I do not find in Hinduism." Many more could give a similar testimony. This is a fact which the contemporary view wholly ignores.

Second, if I water down my convictions about Christ, then I am implicitly suggesting to the other man that he too should reduce his basic convictions. But we are not diplomats, each making concessions across the table in order to reach a compromise. Our convictions are not bargaining counters, they are part of our very being, and are bound up with that loyalty which each of us owes to the best of his past. To renounce that loyalty, or to diminish its significance, is in the end to trivialise ourselves. If in effect I say to men like William Smith, Nehemiah Goreh and J. R. Ballantyne: "You were all mistaken," is it I or they who are diminished? Moreover we have seen that it is the paradox of friendship that though differing convictions may prevent a meeting of minds, they by no means exclude and sometimes even enable a meeting at the level of common humanity. Heart leaps across to heart and there is formed a bond which is all the more precious because its meaning cannot be expressed in words.

I am therefore gripped by two loyalties: to the Christian tradition and all that it has given me, which means supremely Christ himself. All this I must share with others, for that is my missionary vocation. I am also held by loyalty to my friends of other faiths. How can I do justice to this double commitment?

My loyalty to Christ must be open-ended. He is not a formula of which the exact words must be preserved inviolate, but a person in whom I can discover ever new dimensions, not least through my meeting with men of other faiths. It is the will of God that all men should find salvation and so I can and must be confident that my Hindu, Muslim and Buddhist friends are not outside the range of his redeeming love. The God who is utterly Christ-like is continually pressing upon their lives in countless ways, hidden and unrecognised, in the stirrings of conscience, the striving after excellence in their daily work, the growth of compassion for the needy and poor, in the provoking of new questions. If God is present everywhere then he is doing this among all men all the time. For though salvation is through Christ alone, we cannot set limits to the scope of his redemption in places and times where his messengers have not penetrated. At the same time we must be true to our obligation of presenting to and sharing with men the Christ whom they have not yet recognised.

At this point we need to remember that the question of who is or is not saved through Christ is a purely domestic one for Christians. It is of not the slightest interest to Hindus, Muslims or Buddhists. Why should it be? Also, while it is a question which assumes great importance when Christians are talking among themselves, it seems much less important when we actually go out and meet other men. For genuine love demands that I give the other man space to be himself, and allow him to describe himself in his own terms. Do we not all object to being labelled and put into other people's mental pigeon holes? Talking about other men is one thing: actually meeting them is something very different.

There is a comparable difference between theology and worship. In theology we talk about God, bending the minds he has given us to grappling with our questions. This task is necessary but also hazardous for the word 'God' can easily degenerate into an intellectual counter which we push around as in a game. The remedy for this is not less theology but more worship, for in worship God is not the object of our thinking but the subject who comes to meet us in mystery and majesty, transcending all our thoughts and all our language. Similarly, to meet a Hindu or Muslim is to be confronted by the great mystery of another personality. Like worship, this meeting continually reminds us that just because persons are persons they elude all our attempts to contain them in our neat little schemes.

Our conclusion can only be that the question of other men's final destiny is one to which we cannot possibly know the answer. We must be content to leave it where it properly belongs, and that is in the hands of God. Christ's parables of judgment—the sheep and the goats for example—point to a similar conclusion. In the end we shall all be in for a lot of surprises.

This reticence becomes very positive when we remember that the New Testament speaks of a salvation which embraces much more than the destiny of individuals: "He has made known to us his hidden purpose. . . namely, that the universe, all in heaven and all on earth, might be brought into a unity in Christ." (*Ephesians* 1.9-10) In the risen Christ we can see both the pledge and the pattern of that final consummation. In some words which deserve much pondering John Baillie relates the distinctiveness of Christ to that goal of the final unity of all men:

"For if it had been so that each could find God in his own way, each would be finding him without at the same time finding his brother. If the love of God were revealed to each in a different place then we could all meet him without meeting one another in love. If the various tribes of mankind could find their ultimate enlightenment and salvation in different names, the human race would for ever remain divided. Men might still attempt to unite on the level of certain secondary and prudential interests but are we not learning today from bitter experience how fragile and unstable this kind of association must always be, if in their ultimate concern, which is their concern for salvation, men remain apart and strangers from one another".[1]

When strangers have become friends it is possible to discuss some of those searching questions about human values and about the kind of society we want to create and to believe that in doing so we are playing our part in the fulfilment of that great divine purpose.

This brings us to the final question. It is one that every missionary is asked, and one that every man sometimes asks himself, when he stops to look at his life and his work: what is the value of it all? Throughout this book I have set the highest value on personal friendship, yet my Hindu friends are very few, they would by no means agree to the interpretation of our meeting that I have given, and friendship seems a very tender and fragile flower in the midst of the desert wastes that threaten to engulf us all in the last quarter of the 20th century. Not only this, but the practice of Christian friendship is a costly and difficult art in the which I am only a clumsy beginner. Yet even the greatest artists are surprisingly reluctant to claim ultimate value for what they attempt.

T. S. Eliot once wrote:

"As things are, and as fundamentally they must always be, poetry is not a career, but a mug's game. No honest poet can ever feel quite sure of the permanent value of what he has written: he may have wasted his time and messed up his life for nothing."[2]

For Christian faith that is a liberating statement for it delivers us from the disease of self-justification. At the end of the day every missionary knows that he does no more than the widow who dropped her tiny coin into the temple treasury. Yet someone was watching the widow and his word transformed the meaning of her act. The supreme artist gathers up all the broken fragments of work half done, and of work marred by human sin and blindness, and uses them for the completion of that great masterpiece which is the summing up of all things in himself.

"And what you thought you came for
Is only a shell, a husk of meaning
From which the purpose breaks only when it is fulfilled
If at all. Either you had no purpose
Or the purpose is beyond the end you figure
And it is altered in fulfilment."[3]

NOTES

1. C. G. Jung, *Symbols of Transformation* Routledge and Kegan Paul, (Second Edition, 1967) page 235
2. Nirmale Deshpande, *Chingling* (Sarva Seva Sangh Prakashan, Rajghat: Varanasi) page 24

Notes to Chapter 2.
1. *The Church History Association of India* is producing a history of the church in several volumes with the specific purpose of correcting the kind of defects mentioned in this paragraph.
2. *Recollections of an Indian Missionary* and *Further Recollections of an Indian Missionary.*
3. This book was called *Dwij*—'twice born'. Smith published it anonymously and did not mention Goreh by name in it. He wanted to avoid further difficulties for both Goreh and himself with the Hindu community.
4. I owe this information about the three objects for which the Sanskrit University was founded to its present librarian, Dr Lakshmi Narayan Tiwari.
5. Dashashwamedh is the name of the best-known part of the water front on the edge of the Ganges.
6. Quoted in *The Church Missionary Record 1866*, page 373. The remaining quotations in this chapter from William Smith's writings are taken from his papers which are in the archives of the Church Missionary Society. Some of his material is also quoted in M. Shering *The Life and Labours of the Rev William Smith.*

7. C. E. Gardner, *Life of Father Goreh* (1900) page 102
8. Quoted in J. R. Ballantyne, *Christianity Contrasted With Hindu Philosophy* (London 1859) page viii
9. Ibid, page x
10. J. R. Ballantyne, *The Bible for Pundits* (Benares 1860) page xix
11. Ibid, page xl
12. Ibid, page lxxxviii
13. Ibid, pages xcii-xciii
14. The four Vedas, sometimes collectively referred to as the Veda, are the oldest and most sacred of the Hindu scriptures. The orthodox trace all later developments in Hinduism to this source.
15. Professor Hansraj Agarwal, *Sanskrit Sahitya Ka Itihas* (Varanasi, 1965) page 333
16. C. E, Gardner, *op. cit.* page 248
The books mentioned in notes 2, 3, 6 and 7 are available in the library of the Church Missionary Society, London. The two books by J. R. Ballantyne referred to in notes 8-13 are in the library of the Brotherhood of the Ascended Christ, Delhi.

Notes to Chapter 3.
1. T. S. Eliot, *Four Quartets* (Faber and Faber) page 19
2. A *mantra* here means a verse of sacred scripture.

Notes to Chapter 4.
1. T. R. Glover, *The Jesus of History.* page 75
2. This poem can be found in *The Oxford Book of Twentieth Century English Verse* (1973) page 453
3. *Sanskaras* are the influences which a man is believed to inherit from his previous birth. Hindus use this word where we would say heredity.
4. W. H. Auden, *Forewords and Afterwords* (Faber and Faber) page 50
5. The *Mahabharat war* is the theme of the great epic poem of the same name. From childhood all Hindus are familiar with its main incidents and characters.

Notes to Chapter 5.
1. J. Baillie, *The Sense of the Presence of God*, page 208
2. T. S. Eliot, The Use of Poetry (Faber and Faber) page 154
3. T. S. Eliot, Four Quartets (Faber and Faber) page 36